P9-ASF-638

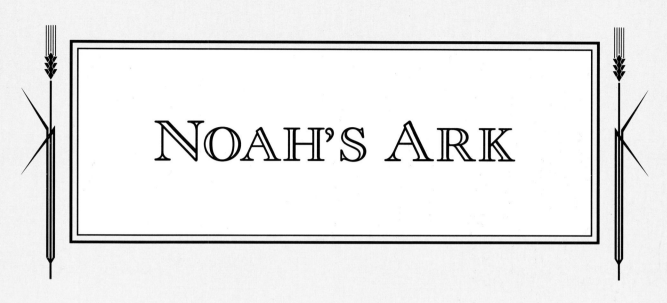

NOAH'S ARK

Louis Weber, C.E.O.
Publications International, Ltd.
7373 North Cicero Avenue
Lincolnwood, Illinois 60646

Manufactured in USA.

8 7 6 5 4 3 2 1

ISBN: 1-56173-718-6

Contributing Writer: Marlene Targ Brill

Consultant: David M. Howard, Jr., Ph.D.

Cover Illustration: Stephen Marchesi

Book Illustrations: Thomas Gianni

David M. Howard, Jr., Ph.D. is an associate professor of Old Testament
and Semitic Languages, and is a member of the Society of Biblical
Literature and the Institute for Biblical Research.

Publications International, Ltd.

One day, many years after God created Adam and Eve, He looked closely at all the people on earth. There were many more people now. They had forgotten about God and His ways.

"I see only evil in people's hearts," God said sadly. "I am sorry that I made them." God grew more and more unhappy about this. He then decided to start all over again.

God had one faithful servant named Noah. Noah and his family loved God. God wanted to save Noah and his family. So, God said to Noah, " I am going to put an end to all things as they are now."

God started to tell Noah about His plan and what He wanted Noah to do. "Build yourself an ark, a large boat of wood. Put many rooms in it." God went on to tell Noah exactly how big to make the ark and why He wanted him to do these things.

"You shall do this because I will cause a great rain to flood the earth. But you and your family shall be safe."

Noah did as God commanded. He built the ark with help from his three sons, Shem, Ham, and Japheth. Noah's neighbors probably thought he was foolish. They could see him and this huge ship he was building in the middle of dry land. What could he be doing?

Meanwhile, God told Noah to bring two of each living thing to the ark. This was a very big job. Noah and his family were going to have to take care of all the animals while they were on the ark. There were big and small animals, strong and weak animals, insects and birds of all kinds. Every type of animal you can think of was going to go on the ark!

Once all the animals were together, God told Noah to take clothing and food for the journey. Some food was for Noah and his family to eat. Some was for the animals. And some was to store for after the flood.

Noah did all that God ordered.

Later, God spoke to Noah again. He said, "Go into the ark now, you and all who are with you. In seven days I will send rain on the earth. The rain will last forty days and forty nights. Water will wash away everything from the ground."

Noah followed God's instructions. He loaded all of the animals into the ark. They had to put all their food and clothes inside the ark. Finally, Noah and his family entered the ark. This was the last time they would be on dry land for a very long time.

On the seventh day, God shut the ark. Rain began to fall to the earth.

At first drops of rain fell here and there. But it was not long before great waves of water pounded the ground. Soon, large puddles formed. Streams turned into rivers. Rivers turned into oceans.

The water began to get higher and higher. Floodwater was so strong it lifted the ark above the earth. People and animals ran for high places. But there seemed to be water everywhere! Soon water covered every tree and mountain top.

Only Noah and those who were with him in the ark had a safe place to stay.

The ark floated along safely. Inside, Noah and his family were safe and warm. They took care of the animals. The rain came down for forty days and forty nights. All that could be seen for miles and miles was water and cloudy skies.

But God had not forgotten about Noah and the good people and creatures on the ark. God caused a strong wind to blow the clouds apart. The rain stopped. A bright sun came out and started to dry up all the floodwaters.

Slowly, little by little, the water went down. Before too long, the tops of mountains could be seen peeking through the water. God caused the ark to rest on top of a mountain called Ararat.

One day, Noah opened the ark window and sent out a raven. The raven saw nothing but water. There was no place for a bird to land. One week later, Noah sent out a dove. The dove had to return to the ark because there still wasn't a place to land.

Noah waited another week and sent the dove out again. This time, the dove came back with a leaf from an olive tree. Noah knew that enough water was gone for trees to grow again.

After one more week, Noah sent the dove out again. This time, it did not return. The bird had found a place to build a nest. Now Noah knew that all of the floodwater had dried up.

Noah removed the door from the ark. Imagine what he saw! There, after such a long time with nothing but water everywhere, Noah could see land! There were mountains and plains, hills and valleys. Even the rivers and lakes were normal again.

Then Noah heard God speak to him. "You have done as I commanded," God said. "Now leave the ark with your family. Bring out all the living things you cared for during the flood. Let them live on earth and grow in numbers."

So Noah and everyone on the ark did as God ordered.

They were all happy to step onto dry land again. They felt thankful that God had taken such good care of them. They wanted to thank God for all these things. So, they built an altar and prayed. They offered their thanks to God for their safety.

God heard Noah's prayers. Right then, God made a promise in His heart:

"I will never destroy the ground because of evil in the human heart. I will never destroy every living creature as I have done. From now on, you will plant seeds and harvest crops. There will be summer and winter and day and night. I will give you everything you need for your family to grow large and strong."

God repeated this promise to Noah. "Never again shall I flood the earth." Then God sent a beautiful rainbow across the sky.

"This first rainbow is a sign of my word. Other rainbows will remind you and all future people of my promise. Whenever a rainbow appears in the clouds, I will see it and remember my promise."